Glacier Travel and Crevasse Rescue

Mountain Focus

CLIMBING - MOUNTAINEERING - SKI TOURING
Instruction & Guiding

www.mountainfocus.info

Glacier Travel and Crevasse Rescue

The Climber's Guide to Accessing Alpine Terrain

Glacier Travel and Crevasse Rescue
The Climber's Guide to Accessing Alpine Terrain
First Paperback Edition

ISBN: 9798641119205

Published and Distributed by Amazon Kindle Direct Publishing.

Writers:
Mike Thomas
Neil Chelton

Illustrator:
Neil Chelton

Photographers:
- Alex Ratson
- Mike Thomas
- Maria Parkes
- Ronnie Legg
- Petrouchka Steiner-Grierson

Front Cover: Ryan Larkin on Serratus Mountain, Tantalus Range, Canada.
Photographer: Alex Ratson

Warning: Mountains are Dangerous!
This book is intended for people who are competent at basic mountaineering skills such as:
- Wearing a harness
- Tying into a rope
- Belaying
- Understanding mountain hazards and weather
- Having a good knowledge of first aid

This book is designed to be supplemented with practical instruction from qualified professionals. Do not rely on it as your primary source of glacier travel information. If you are unsure about any of the information given in this book, it is strongly recommended that you seek qualified instruction. Failure to do this may result in serious injury or death. The writers and employees of VDiff disclaim all responsibility and liability for any injuries or losses incurred by any person participating in the activities described in this book.

Contents

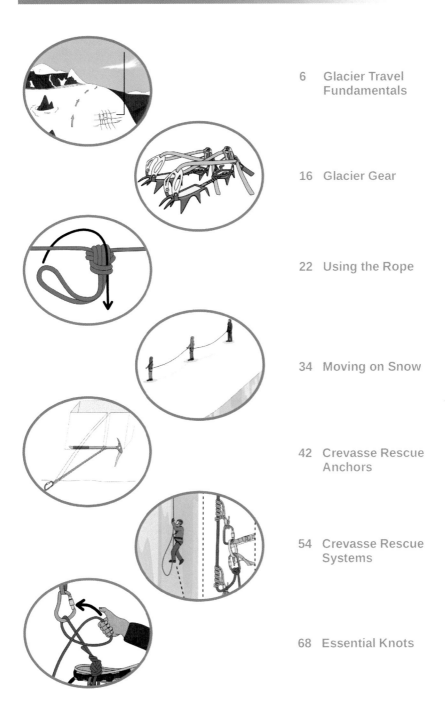

Ryan Larkin at Joffre Lakes Provincial Park, BC, Canada. 📷 Alex Ratson.

Glacier Travel Fundamentals

Introduction

Travelling on a glacier is an exciting element of exploring the high mountains. Many alpine rock climbs can only be accessed by travelling across glaciers, or the glacier itself may be the best route to an alluring summit. Before stepping onto a glacier, it is important to learn how to safely negotiate their hazards.

What is a Glacier?

A glacier is a mass of consolidated snow and ice which flows very slowly down a mountain.

Different parts of a glacier move at different speeds, similar to the flow rate of water in a river — faster at the center and surface, slower at the sides and bottom where bedrock creates friction.

Glacial flow fractures the surface of the ice, creating large cracks (crevasses) which can be up to 45 meters deep, 20 meters wide and hundreds of meters long.

Crevasses are the main hazard to people wishing to cross a glacier.

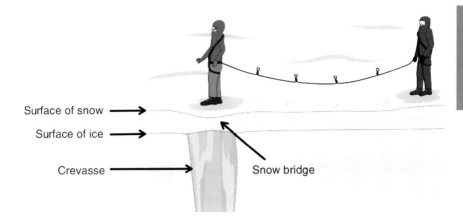

Surface of snow ⟶

Surface of ice ⟶

Crevasse ⟶   Snow bridge

Dry Glaciers

You will encounter dry glaciers in summer, particularly at lower altitudes, when the winter snow has melted and bare ice is exposed.

Because dry glaciers are completely free of snow, it is possible to see all the crevasses and therefore much easier to pick a route to avoid them.

A dry glacier in Svalbard. 📷 Ronnie Legg.

Wet Glaciers

Wet glaciers are snow-covered and much more dangerous. The snow does not fill the crevasses, but instead forms a layer on the surface which hides them.

The layer of snow covering a crevasse is known as a snow bridge.

Snow Bridges

A snow bridge can be thick, well frozen and strong enough to support the weight of a person.

Or it could be thin, unfrozen and weak, allowing an unsuspecting climber to fall through into the crevasse beneath. Because of this, it is very important to be roped up as part of a team to help reduce the consequences of falling into a crevasse.

Snow bridges are at their strongest early in the morning when the snow is well frozen. Remember this when you're following your footprints back later in the afternoon.

A wet glacier in Greenland. Maria Parkes.

Crevasses

Although crevasses could be almost anywhere and orientated in any direction, there are certain parts of a glacier where they are more commonly found. Crevasses often form:

At the top edge of the glacier, known as a bergschrund

On undulations where the angle of the slope increases significantly

Around bedrock features, such as a nunatak (rock tower)

On the outside edge of a turn

When the distance between valley walls narrows or expands

Where two glaciers meet

Points of Stress and Compression

As the ice moves over undulations and around corners, points of stress are created on the outside edge, causing the ice to rip apart and form crevasses.

These cracks in the ice typically (but not always) run perpendicular to the flow of the glacier.

Points of compression are created on the inside edges where ice is being pushed together. These areas have the least number of crevasses and usually present the safest route to travel.

This is easier to understand if you imagine bending a Mars Bar. Cracks form on the outside of the bend, and chocolate is pushed together on the inside edge.

Finding Crevasses

The first step in choosing a route across a glacier is to figure out where the crevasses are. Here are some tips:

- Study photographs of the glacier before the trip, as some crevasse patterns remain the same year after year.
- On the approach, try to get a good look at the glacier before you reach it. A maze is much easier to negotiate when viewed from outside than from within.
- Look out for sagging trenches on the surface of the snow. Snow covering a large crevasse gradually deforms and sags under its own weight.
- Probe suspect areas using an axe or ski pole (with the basket removed). Push the shaft of the axe into the snow with a smooth motion. If there is suddenly less resistance, you have most likely found a hole.
- If you find a crevasse, there are probably more nearby.

Other Glacier Hazards

Seracs

A serac is a block or column of glacial ice often formed:
- Where two crevasses intersect
- At the lower end of a glacier
- Where a glacier steepens dramatically

Seracs are dangerous because they can collapse with no warning. If you are below them, you could be hit by ice blocks.

Rockfall

Rockfall is a hazard if travelling on glaciers bordered by steep mountains, or when climbing on rock faces. Rockfall is reduced overnight when the cold temperatures freeze rock in place.

The most dangerous times to be exposed to this risk are late morning when direct sunlight melts the bonds between ice and rock, and also in the evenings when meltwater freezes and expands.

Exposure to Seracs and Rockfall

The only way to increase safety when travelling beneath seracs or potential rockfall is to reduce the amount of time you are exposed to the risk. Either alter your route or move efficiently without stopping to minimize the exposure. Factor this in when planning your climb.

Avalanches

Reaching an alpine climbing objective can involve travelling on snow slopes which are prone to avalanches. Avalanche hazard is a complex subject and is not covered in this manual. An excellent resource is *Staying Alive in Avalanche Terrain* by Bruce Tremper.

Whiteouts

When fog or cloud descend on a glacier, snow and sky become one indistinguishable blur of white, with no apparent up or down.

Travelling on complicated glaciated terrain in poor visibility can be very serious, as making the correct route choice can be nearly impossible.

Even if the weather is clear on the approach, it is worth tracking your route via GPS, so if clouds close in during the day, you will be able to follow your path back.

Assessing Hazards

With all of these dangers, you may be wondering how anyone has ever survived a glacier crossing!

While there are many hazards, there are also many ways of reducing your exposure to them. This mostly boils down to:

- Prior planning (bring the right gear and study maps of your intended route beforehand).
- Waiting for the correct weather and conditions.
- Practising skills (see next page).
- Making decisions based on facts, rather than emotions (don't be afraid of turning back if it's too dangerous, even if you *want* to continue).

Training

Training for glacier travel means practising the techniques described in this book. Plenty of practise is essential.

Skills such as prusiking out of a crevasse or hauling someone out are strenuous, slow and clunky at first, but with practise you'll develop a slick and fast technique.

You should aim to reach a level of competence where your snow anchors are always bomber and you can set up any crevasse rescue system quickly and efficiently.

Always practise in a group and tell someone at home where you are going.

What To Practise

Skill	Practised once	Practised a few times	Competent
Tying into the end of the rope and taking coils	☐	☐	☐
Tying into the middle of the rope	☐	☐	☐
Measuring the rope accurately with arm spans	☐	☐	☐
Tying jamming knots	☐	☐	☐
Moving on snow of different angles using an ice axe and crampons	☐	☐	☐
Snow probing	☐	☐	☐
Wearing the right clothing in different temperatures and conditions	☐	☐	☐
Moving together with a taut rope	☐	☐	☐
Various methods of crossing crevasses	☐	☐	☐
Self-arresting in different positions	☐	☐	☐
Making snow and ice anchors in different conditions	☐	☐	☐
Prusiking out of a crevasse	☐	☐	☐
Hauling a victim out of a crevasse	☐	☐	☐
Navigating in poor weather	☐	☐	☐
Map reading and planning a safe route	☐	☐	☐

Easier Skills ... *Harder Skills*

Where To Practise

It's important to build up your experience progressively with regards to terrain.

The ideal venue to have your first practise sessions is on a low-angled, non-glacial snow slope which has a safe runout and zero risk of:

- Avalanches
- Crevasses
- Rockfall
- Seracs

Find a safe windscoop to simulate a crevasse, or take some shovels and dig a hole.

Once you have built up some skills, progress to a simple glacier which has easy access. Go in a large group for increased safety and fun.

With the experience gained from easier terrain, you can then travel on more complicated glaciers. Only head off on remote, gnarly glacial adventures once you have gained enough real experience.

After each session, review what worked and what didn't. Focus on improving the things you found most difficult.

As with anything worthwhile, it will take time to build up a good level of competence. Trying to shortcut this process is extremely dangerous and will probably result in disaster.

Once you have practised and become competent at the skills listed on the previous page, you will be ready to do your first real glacier crossing.

It is recommended that at least one member of the team has plenty of glacier travel experience, because it takes many glacier crossings to build up skills such as spotting crevasses and other hazards, and negotiating a route through them.

Big crevasse on the Coleman Glacier, Mount Baker, Washington. Petrouchka Steiner-Grierson

Dent du Géant, European Alps. Mike Thomas.

Glacier Gear

Gear

Glacier Gear

What gear you take on the glacier will depend entirely on what you plan to do once across it.

The list below covers equipment that is recommended for the glacier crossing itself. You will obviously need extra equipment if planning a rock climb or an overnight camp.

Clothing

Glaciers can present extremes of temperature. On a clear summer's day, it can feel like you're standing on an inescapable boiling hot mirror, as the sun reflects off the snow and burns the underside of your nose.

Conversely, when the clouds roll in and the wind picks up, it's like being inside a giant fridge-freezer.

In a rescue situation, you may be standing around for hours in these conditions. It's important to bring the correct clothing so you can withstand this variable climate.

The clothing system in this chapter is for typical summer alpinism and will need to be adjusted to be warmer or lighter for specific objectives or different times of year.

Upper Body
Wear layers that you can easily adjust for different temperatures, as differences throughout the day can be huge.

The layering system starts with a long-sleeved base layer (wool is ideal). It helps to protect you from the sun when worn on its own and wicks sweat away from your skin.

A mid-weight fleece (preferably with a hood) can be worn over your base layer, with a waterproof jacket on the top. This will keep the wind, rain or snow off when necessary.

These three layers combined are a reasonably warm 'active' set up for an average summer alpine environment.

Spare Warm Layer

This is a layer that you will only wear on windy summits, long lunch breaks or during rescue situations.

Down jackets are excellent in dry climates below freezing and are very lightweight for their warmth. Puffy synthetic jackets are much better in warmer weather, especially if rain is forecast.

Some down jackets will repel a small amount of moisture, but the feathers will clump together in a rain storm and then you'll freeze.

Legs

Mid-weight soft shell trousers are the best choice. They are breathable, fast drying, offer some wind resistance and can shed a bit of snow.

It's also important to carry a pair of lightweight waterproof over-trousers. These will add warmth if necessary and provide protection from wind, snow and rain.

Thermal leggings can be worn under these layers to add warmth in colder weather.

Extremities

Good quality wool socks are warm and help prevent blisters.

A windproof woollen hat is small and lightweight for the amount of warmth it provides. Keep it in your pocket when not in use so you can adjust temperature quickly without going into your rucksack.

Take a pair of thin gloves that you can handle the rope with (close fitting leather gloves are good) and a thicker pair to wear if these get wet or the temperature drops.

Boots

You will need stiff mountaineering boots which are crampon compatible — either B2 or B3 mountain boots. Which type you choose depends on what else you'll be using them for. B2's are lighter, making them the best choice for general alpinism and summer rock scrambling. B3's are heavier, warmer and more suitable if you plan to use them for ice climbing too.

Short gaiters are worn over your boots to stop snow entering into the top of them.

Snow Climbing Equipment

Crampons

Any pair of 12-point crampons will be suitable to cross a low-angled glacier. Crampons improve traction on hard snow or ice, but are less useful in softer snow.

It is standard practice to wear crampons at all times when roped together on a glacier. Without them, you're unlikely to hold a falling climber.

Axe

A straight-shafted 50-60cm ice axe is a good choice for general alpinism.

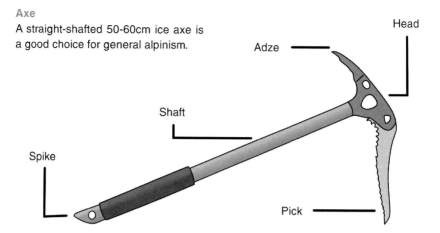

Head

Adze

Shaft

Spike

Pick

Poles

Adjustable ski or trekking poles provide extra balance when travelling on low-angled glaciers where an axe is too short to reach the ground. They are also useful for probing crevasses.

Poles can be compressed and stored on the outside of your rucksack when not in use.

Skis

Skis are only recommended for glacier travel if each member of the team is a competent skier.

Techniques such as self arresting and keeping the rope taut when moving downhill are difficult for most skiers, and will be impossible for newbies.

Crevasse Rescue Rack

Each climber should keep the following gear clipped to their harness:
- 4x screwgate carabiners
- 2x snapgate carabiners
- 2x prusik cords
- 2x ice screws (medium to long size)
- 1x 120cm sling
- 1x 30cm sling
- 1x locking pulley (optional)

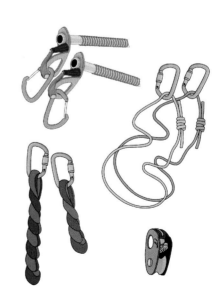

Prusik Length

Prusiks are commonly made from 120cm of 5mm cord tied into a loop using a double fisherman's bend (see page 75). This creates a finished loop of around 45cm.

Other Personal Equipment

Each climber should also bring:

- 40-litre rucksack
- Harness
- Helmet
- Headlamp with spare batteries
- Sun protection (sunscreen, category 3 or 4 sunglasses, lip balm, hat)
- Emergency blizzard bag
- Food
- Water bottle (1 litre is generally fine if there are streams to resupply, otherwise bring more)

Group Equipment

Each group should carry:

- Rope (a 50 meter single rope, 9mm in diameter with dry treatment is a good choice for summer alpine use, though this may change depending on your specific objective)
- 1st aid kit
- Navigation (map, compass and GPS)
- Communication (mobile or sat phone with relevant rescue numbers)
- Group shelter
- Spare headlamp
- V-thread tool
- Small repair kit (duck tape, short pieces of wire, knife, thin cord)

The Darwin Icefall, Haupapa Tasman Glacier, New Zealand. Petrouchka Steiner-Grierson

Approaching the summit of an unknown peak, Liverpool Land, Greenland. Neil Chelton.

Using the Rope

Using the Rope

It can be tempting to cross a glacier without bothering to get the rope out, especially if it looks easy or if other climbers have crossed without problems before.

This attitude is extremely dangerous. Not being roped up will greatly reduce the chance of being rescued from a glacier's main hazard — falling into a crevasse.

The process of roping up is:
1) Two climbers tie into the ends of the rope.
2) The appropriate length of rope is measured between climbers.
3) The middle climbers tie in (for a team of three or four) or jamming knots are tied (for a team of two).
4) Chest coils are taken with the extra rope.

Each of these steps are described in detail in this chapter.

Group Size

A roped team of three is a standard size for travel on a non-technical glacier. It is safer than a team of two (with an extra climber to hold a fall) and easier to manage than a team of four. Never travel on a glacier alone.

Two or more independent teams is beneficial (e.g; six climbers split into two teams of three). If a team is involved in an accident, they will have backup help.

Glacier travel is very risky for a team of two if no other roped teams are nearby. The climber who stops the fall must build an anchor while in the arrest position, set up a hauling system and complete the entire rescue by themselves.

In this scenario, it is essential that both climbers are proficient at crevasse rescue.

Rope Length

The minimum length of rope required for glacier travel is:

- 40 meters for a team of two
- 50 meters for a team of three or four

Tying Into the End of the Rope

The rethreaded figure-8 is widely recognised as being the safest way to connect the end of the rope to your harness (see page 71).

The climbers who tie into the end will also take chest coils (see page 30).

Measuring the Rope

Climbers should tie into the rope at certain distances from each other. This spaces people far enough apart so that when crossing a typical crevasse, only one person is at risk of falling in at any time. A general guide of the minimum distances are given below.

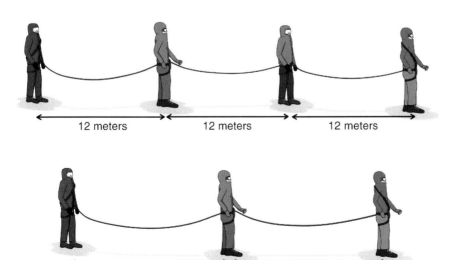

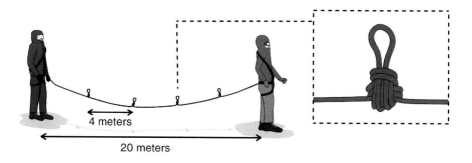

4 meters

20 meters

Being closer than these recommended minimums is dangerous because it puts the whole team at risk of falling into the same crevasse. Consider tying in with more distance on glaciers that may have bigger crevasses.

Basically, being further apart is safer. The only downsides of being far apart is that communication can become harder and it is more difficult to keep the rope taut.

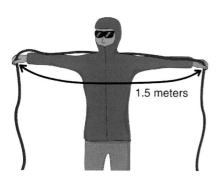

1.5 meters

Arm Spans

The distance of rope is easily measured using arm spans. For many people, a double arm span of rope is about 1.5 meters (check this beforehand and adjust your calculation as necessary).

Remember that 1.5 meters of rope (1 span) is used when tying into the middle or when tying a jamming knot.

For example, a team of two climbers need to be 20 meters apart (approx 13 spans) with 4 jamming knots (4 spans). So a total of 17 spans of rope must be measured.

Tying Into the Middle

The remaining climbers in a three or four person team must tie into the middle of the rope. This will be the very middle in a team of three (a rope with a middle marker helps). For a team of four, the middle two climbers will be evenly spaced from the rope's center.

Step 1

Tie an overhand knot with a long bight of rope, from waist height to the floor.

Step 2

Tie a second overhand 6 inches down from the first.

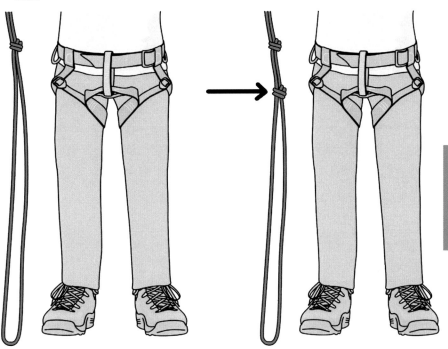

Step 3

Thread the bight through your harness and back through the overhand knot as shown.

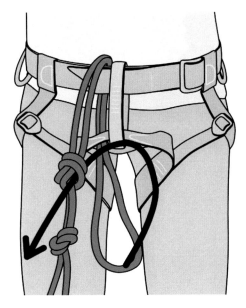

Step 4
Tie a stopper knot.

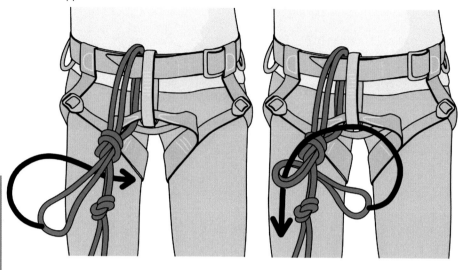

Step 5
Clip the tail back to your belay loop with a screwgate carabiner.

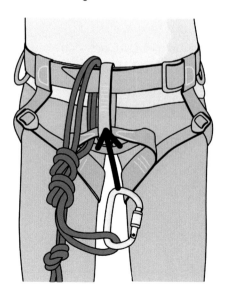
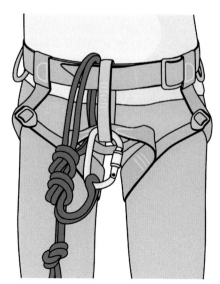

Jamming Knots

It will be very challenging to hold the weight of a falling climber when travelling in a team of two. To help with this, you should tie jamming knots in the rope.

During a fall, the rope cuts through the snow on the lip of the crevasse, creating a slot which the knot (hopefully) jams into.

This knot won't hold the fall by itself — it merely adds some friction which assists the climber in arresting the fall. Knots should be tied at 4 meter intervals.

Step 1
Tie a figure-8 on a bight, with a 60cm long loop.

Step 2
Pull the bight around the back of the knot and though the figure-8 as shown.

Step 3
Do this again, twice more, to create a large jamming knot.

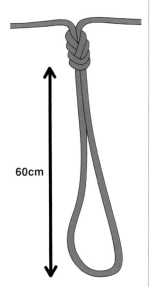

60cm

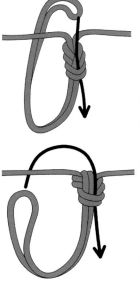

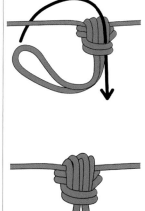

Jamming knots add complications during a crevasse rescue. In a team of two, it is still worth having the knots and then dealing with the extra problem of passing them during a rescue.

Without the knots, both climbers are much more likely to end up in the crevasse, which is a far worse situation! In a larger group, with more climbers to hold the fall, it is usually better to travel without jamming knots.

Chest Coils

When travelling in alpine terrain, it is often preferable for the rope to be shorter than its full length.

A good way to achieve this is for the climber at each end of the rope to use chest coils. This keeps the rope easily accessible in the event of a rescue, and also means the length of rope can be adjusted quickly if needed.

Taking the Coils Off
Reverse this process, taking the coils off one at a time. If you take them all off at once and drop them in the snow, it will make the most epic tangle!

Step 1
Tie in with a neat figure-8 and put your jacket hood up.

Step 2
Take the rope straight up the right side of your chest and around your neck, making sure the rope is snug, not slack.

Step 3
With your left hand held at waist height, coil the rope between your neck and left hand, making sure each coil is of equal length and tension.

Keep taking coils until the desired length of rope remains between you and your partner.

Step 4

Put your left arm through the coils, so they hang on your right shoulder across your body.

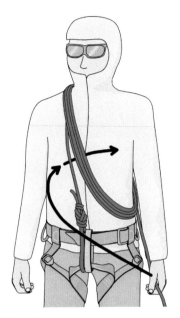

Step 5

With your left hand, reach through the coils and behind the initial vertical strand and grab the live rope. Pull this back out through the coils until you have a 40cm bight of rope.

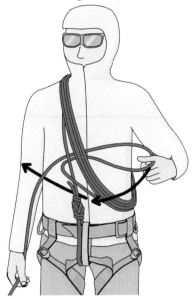

Step 6

Tie this bight of rope in an overhand knot, incorporating the live rope as shown. If the coils are tied correctly, you should be able to pull the live rope without getting strangled.

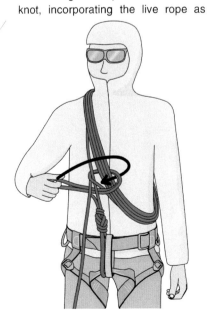

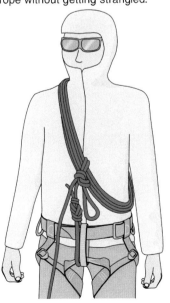

Step 7

Clip the remaining bight of rope to your belay loop.

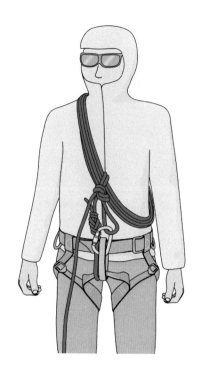

Step 8

Tie a clove hitch on the live rope and clip it to your belay loop. This redirects the pull from chest height down to waist height, meaning that if your partner falls in a crevasse, you stand a better chance of holding the fall and not being pulled over head first!

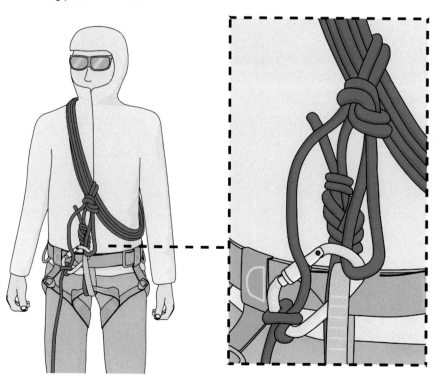

Ropework Tips

Travel Perpendicular
Travelling with the rope at 90 degrees to crevasses only exposes one climber at a time to the hazard of falling into the crevasse. If the rope is running parallel to a crevasse, the whole team risks falling in at the same time!

Roping Up on a Dry Glacier
Moving together while roped up on a dry glacier (one that is completely free of snow) can be more dangerous than going un-roped. Arresting a fall on hard ice is nearly impossible and will likely result in broken ankles and more climbers in the crevasse.

However, when crossing crevasses on a dry glacier, consider making an anchor and belaying each other across.

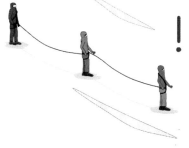

Experience
Ideally, the most experienced mountaineer who is the best at spotting crevasses and choosing a route through them should be at the front.

Tight Rope
Keep the rope tight between each person at all times to reduce shock loading. Not only would a climber fall further if the rope is slack, but it will be much harder for the climber on the surface to hold the fall.

Weight Differences
If there is a significant weight difference between climbers, the lighter climber should be in the down slope position, so that gravity assists them when trying to hold the fall of the heavier climber.

Crossing Nokkedal glacier on skis, Greenland. 📷 Neil Chelton

Moving on Snow

Moving on Snow

The snow which covers a glacier is very variable. Sometimes a 20 degree slope is easy to walk up, with the front team member kicking in steps as they go. On the same slope at other times, you'll be wallowing in powder up to your armpits, or using crampons to front-point up snow which is as hard as ice. Or maybe the snow has transformed and you'll actually be on ice.

It's important to learn how to move on all snow types and how to regain control if you start sliding down a slope.

Kicking Steps
If the snow is hard, the front climber will need to kick steps to create an easy path for the rest of the team. Steps that are slightly incut will be more secure.

When following, kick into the steps to improve them. Simply standing in them is not as stable.

Note
Travelling on snow slopes steeper than 30 degrees requires more advanced mountaineering skills, such as placing lead protection in different snow types and understanding avalanche hazards. These topics are not covered in this guide.

Moving on Low-Angled Snow
Travelling across a fairly flat glacier is simple — just walk and try not to trip over your crampons. But as the slope increases, you will need to adapt your walking technique from what you normally use on city streets.

Hold the axe in your uphill hand and place the shaft into the snow above you. Then move your feet up, one at a time, and repeat. The axe provides balance while you walk uphill — a bit like holding onto a railing when walking up stairs.

Carrying an Ice Axe

In Your Hand
Hold the axe in your hand with your thumb under the adze and the pick pointing back as shown. This means you are always ready for self-arrest if you slip.

On Your Rucksack
If the axe is not needed for a while, attach it securely to the axe-loop on the outside of your bag, as shown below.

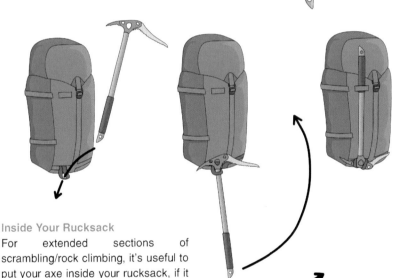

Inside Your Rucksack
For extended sections of scrambling/rock climbing, it's useful to put your axe inside your rucksack, if it will fit. This means it is much less likely to get snagged on something.

On a Shoulder Strap
If you need both hands free, you can quickly store your axe down the back of your rucksack so the pick rests on a shoulder strap.

Simply poke the shaft a few inches under your shoulder strap by your collar bone and raise the head of the axe so the shaft levers off your shoulder.

Then allow the axe to slot down between your back and rucksack.

Tips:
- If this feels uncomfortable, try loosening your shoulder straps a little.
- If you have chest coils on, use the shoulder strap on the same side as the coils.
- If the shaft of the axe is curved, try putting the axe in with the pick facing the other way so the end of the shaft doesn't stick out as much.
- If you take your bag off, remember that the axe isn't attached!

Self-Arrest

The self-arrest technique is used to stop yourself sliding on snow. The simplest scenario is when sliding on your stomach, feet pointing downhill. The correct body position is:

- Axe held diagonally across your body.

- Adze pressed into the hollow below your collar bone (if you don't keep the adze at your shoulder, the pick will be unlikely to bite. It would also be difficult to hold onto the axe if the pick did bite).

- One hand over the head of the axe, the other covering the spike on the end of the shaft (to prevent it from accidentally catching in the snow and being ripped out of your hands or spinning you).

- Face turned away from the axe (in case the pick hits something and the adze kicks back and cuts your nose off, like Joe Simpson).

- Elbows tightly tucked in by your sides (stronger position).

- Legs apart and bent at the knees with feet up in the air (this provides stability and having your crampons in the air prevents them from catching and sending you into a cartwheel).

Once in this position, focus all of your weight over your shoulder and down through the adze to push the pick into the snow. If you don't stop, just keep trying and try harder. At least it will slow you down.

Sliding on Your Back

If you are sliding on your back then you must roll over.

It is best to roll over in the direction of the pick, as this reduces the chance of the spike on the shaft jabbing into the snow by accident.

Sliding Head First

If you are sliding head first you must hold the axe far out to one side, push it into the snow and allow your legs to swing around below you.

Then remove the pick from the snow, bring the axe down to your shoulder and get into the correct position described on the previous page.

Practise

The self-arrest technique needs to be practised to a point where it becomes an instinctive reaction. Try it out on slopes of different angles and snow conditions, making sure there is a safe runout below you. When you need to arrest for real, it must be executed instantly to be most effective.

Crossing Crevasses

There are a few different ways of getting past a crevasse.

In order of preference, these are:
- Go around the end
- Cross on a snow bridge
- Jump over
- Climb inside / abseil over

Going Around

This is the preferred method, since you are much less likely to fall in. Crevasses generally narrow towards their ends, but the visible end may not be the actual end.

Probe carefully and give the end a lot of space. Look for other nearby crevasses and consider if one of them is actually an extension of this crevasse — you might be crossing a snow bridge.

Crossing a Snow Bridge

The strength of a snow bridge varies considerably with temperature — stronger when frozen overnight and weaker in the midday sun. Just because there are footprints on it doesn't mean it won't collapse under your weight.

If you're unsure of the bridge's stability, make a snow anchor and belay across. Once the leader is across, the rest of the team should follow their footprints exactly.

Jumping Over

Jumping over a deep void in the ground is exhilarating and makes you look like a hero on photos. But it can also be very dangerous.

With a solid belay, probe around to find the true edge of the crevasse. Pack down the snow to create a runway for your leap of faith. Make sure to have enough slack rope to complete the jump and keep your axe in the self-arrest position so you can climb up if you land on the lip. The leader then belays the other team members across.

Climbing Inside

Sometimes it may be possible to climb inside a crevasse, walk across the bottom and climb up the adjacent wall. This really only works in shallow crevasses which have easy exits.

Before going in, make sure the bottom of the crevasse really is the bottom and not just a half-sunk snow bridge. As with jumping across, this can be dangerous and requires a solid belay.

Abseiling Over

It is fairly common to abseil over the bergschrund when descending onto the top of a glacier. This is best done from rock anchors (if available), but an anchor could also be made on ice (using a v-thread) or on snow (using a snow bollard) if necessary.

Remember to abseil with a prusik and keep your ice axes handy as you may need to climb up and out of the other side of the crevasse.

Dynamic Risk Assessment

It is important to understand the risks involved in all types of climbing and mountaineering. The process of evaluating these risks during the activity is often referred to as a *dynamic risk assessment*.

When looking at a situation, think about the *likelihood* of a negative incident occurring (e.g: a slip or fall, a hold snapping off, a storm coming in, a rock falling from above), then think about the *consequences* of this happening. How does the terrain, situation or weather affect the consequences of the negative incident?

For example, there might be no serious consequence for a climber who slips on a small snow slope which has a safe runout. Whereas the same incident on a similar slope but with a rocky runout, or a cliff or crevasse below, may lead to serious injury.

It is the relationship between likelihood and consequence that is crucial to evaluating the risks. To stay safe in the mountains we need to continually make these dynamic risk assessments and adjust our plan, or the technique and tactics we use. This will mitigate either the likelihood or consequence to bring risk to an acceptable level for each given situation. Keep asking yourself, *"what will happen if…?"*

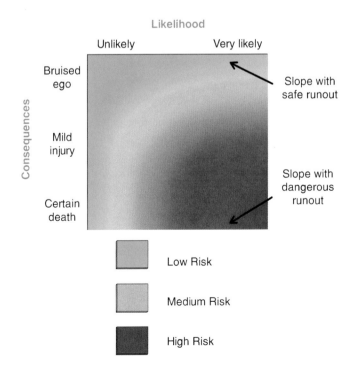

Heavily crevassed glacier near Squamish, BC, Canada. Alex Ratson.

Crevasse Rescue Anchors

Crevasse Rescue Anchors

You will need to make an anchor on the glacier when:
- Performing a crevasse rescue
- Belaying/ abseiling across a crevasse or other tricky ground

Snow Quality
The strength of a snow anchor varies dramatically depending on the snow type. For example; an ice axe buried in powder snow will be useless, whereas the same axe buried in hard snow will be bomber. With good judgement of the snowpack, the anchors described in this chapter will be sufficient for their intended use. However, this judgement is only developed with plenty of practice and experimentation in a safe environment.

Surface Area
Generally, anchors with a bigger surface area are stronger. An ice axe can work well in hard snow, but will not provide sufficient surface area for a secure anchor in soft, unconsolidated snow. A better alternative in this case is to bury a rucksack or a ski (see page 47).

Note
The anchors described in this chapter are made using equipment that you already have with you — ice axe, rucksack or ice screws.

Anchors can also be made from gear which is designed as lead protection in snow, such as pickets or flukes. However, it is assumed that you do not have these more specialized items with you.

Be Precise
Precision is everything with snow anchors. A precise and well constructed anchor can be quite strong, with a sloppy one in the same snow being weak.

It's better to take a little longer making a good anchor that works, rather than rush one which fails halfway through a rescue.

Ice Axe Anchor

Step 1
Use your pick to score a horizontal line in the snow exactly perpendicular to the direction of pull and slightly longer than the length of your ice axe.

It is important not to disturb the snow in the area immediately in front of your anchor as this is where its strength comes from.

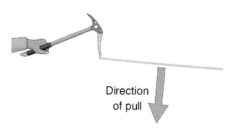

Direction of pull

Front View

Step 2
Cut out a slot in the snow, using the initial scored line as a guide. 30cm is the minimum depth in firm, consolidated snow. If the snow is soft, you may need to dig deeper to find more consolidated snow.

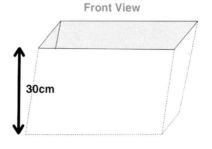

30cm

Make the front face of the slot uniform and slightly incut in relation to the direction of pull. This helps the axe to pull into the snow when weighted, rather than up and out.

Side View

Step 3
Find the centre of mass on the ice axe. Not the middle of the axe, but the middle of the surface area. This is typically about ⅔ of the way along the shaft, towards the head. Mark where this point would be on the slot you have cut in the snow. Cut a narrow slot at this point using the pick and spike of the axe.

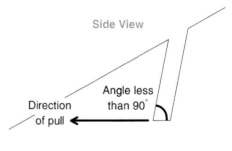

Angle less than 90°

Direction of pull

This slot only needs to be wide enough for a fabric sling, but deep enough so that it reaches to the very base of the horizontal slot. It must also be long enough so that when the sling is attached, the angle created pulls the axe into the snow, not upwards.

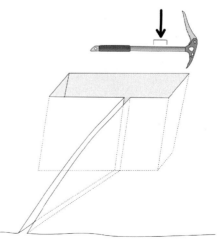

Anchors

Step 4

Clovehitch a 120cm sling around the shaft of the axe at the previously identified point.

Then flip one strand of the sling over the shaft as shown. This causes the clovehitch to tighten up around the shaft when weighted.

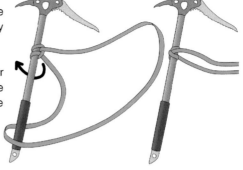

Step 5

Place the axe in the slot horizontally, with the pick facing down and the shaft securely up against the front face at the very base of the slot. Make sure the sling runs through the narrow slot.

Step 6

Backfill the slot with snow and compact it down. Be careful not to disturb the snow in front of the anchor. In some snow types this adds considerable strength to the anchor.

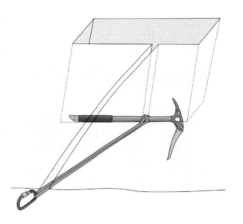

Step 7

Use the anchor with caution and avoid shock loading.

Reinforced Buried Axe

If you have a second axe available, you can slide it in front of the other axe, between the sling's strands to reinforce it. This adds more surface area and improves the anchor's strength.

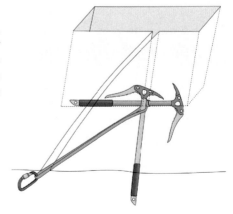

Anchors in Softer Snow

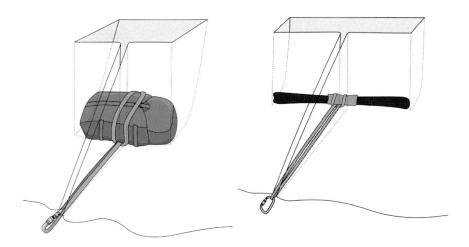

Anchors which are more suitable in softer snow include a buried rucksack or horizontal ski, with a sling girth-hitched around it.

The principles of these anchors are the same as for burying an ice axe, but the item must be buried deeper.

If you are using a ski, be careful to protect the sling from the ski's sharp edges — these could cut the sling.

Position the base of the ski against the front face of the horizontal slot as shown below, and pad the sling with something if possible.

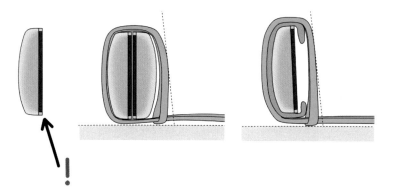

Ice Screw Anchor

You can make an ice screw anchor on a dry glacier, or you might be able to dig through snow on a wet glacier to reach ice.

Step 1 — Clear
Clear away any surface snow and aerated surface ice and get down to good solid glacial ice.

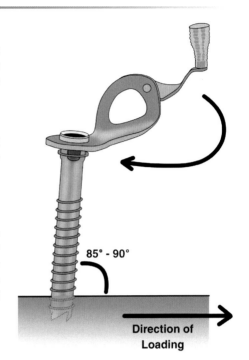

Step 2 — Position
Position the screw perpendicular to the surface of the ice, or slightly towards the direction of loading. Push the screw against the surface while turning it a few times with your wrist until it bites.

85° - 90°

Direction of Loading

Step 3 — Insert
Using the handle, wind the screw all the way into the ice.

Placement Quality
You will get feedback about the quality of the placement as the screw is winding into the ice. Here are some things to consider:

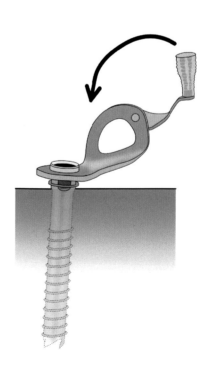

- Feel the resistance of the screw cutting through the ice. Has it gone into an air pocket?
- Look at the core of ice coming out of the back of the screw. In good glacier ice this should come out looking like a crumpled ice cigar! Poorer quality placements will have snow, slush or nothing at all coming out of the hole.
- Look at the surface of the ice around the screw. Is it cracking? Some small surface cracks are okay but large sections of the ice cracking are not good.

Step 4 — Loading Direction

You need to finish with the hanger pointing in the direction of pull.

Do not force the hanger around — it is better to unwind slightly to get the hanger pointing in the correct direction. Forcing it would start to strip the threads of the ice screw placement.

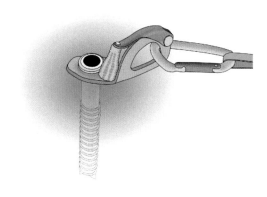

Step 5 — Double Up

A 16cm screw in good ice will hold around 10kN — the same as an average cam in good rock.

If possible, place two screws at least 30cm apart and offset. Equalize them with a sling to create an anchor.

Abalakov Thread (V-Thread)

A V-thread is an ice anchor that is often used for abseiling.

You Will Need

- a long ice screw (21cm)
- a length of 7mm cord
- a V-thread tool

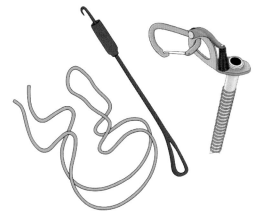

Anchors

Step 1

Clear the surface so you get to solid ice. Place the ice screw perpendicular to the ice, but at a 60 degree angle sideways. Pay attention to the quality of the ice as the screw is being placed. It needs to be good.

Step 2

Remove the screw.

Step 3

Make a second hole at a distance approximately equal to the length of the screw so that you end up with an equilateral triangle. It helps to look down the first hole to aim the second screw placement.

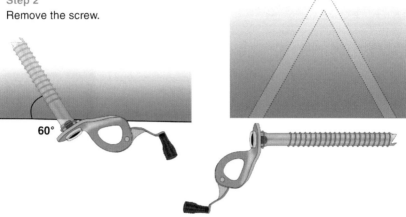

Step 4

Clean out the holes with your V-thread tool. With the tool at the bottom of the first hole, poke the cord into the second hole.

As the cord passes through into the first hole, hook it with the tool and pull it out.

Step 5

Tie both ends of the cord together using a double fisherman's bend. Make sure the loop is not too tight — the angle when weighting the loop should be around 45 degrees.

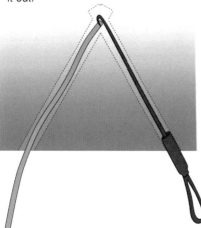

Notes

- As with all ice anchors, the quality of the ice has a massive impact on the strength of the anchor. A well constructed V-thread in good ice will hold around 8kN.

- V-threads can be made in a horizontal or vertical plain. Some evidence shows that vertical V-threads are slightly stronger, but many people find these to be trickier to construct accurately.

- It's important to have an accurate construction — with the angles at 60 degrees and having the connection of the two holes at the maximum depth.

- If in doubt, make two V-threads (more than 30cm apart) and link them together to make an equalised anchor.

V-Thread Without Cord

To make a V-thread anchor without cord, simply poke the climbing rope through the holes instead of the cord. If abseiling on two ropes, it is important that the joining knot is positioned a good distance away so it does not get pulled into the hole. This will create an unusual strain on the anchor.

It is possible for the rope to become stuck if it freezes in place. The last person down should check that the rope slides before they abseil.

Back-Up Your Anchor

To secure the first person's descent, the V-thread can be combined with another ice screw. Connect this back-up screw to the rope with a little slack so it isn't actually weighted when the first person abseils. Make sure there isn't too much slack, as this would shock-load the backup screw if the V-thread failed. The last person then removes the ice screw before they descend.

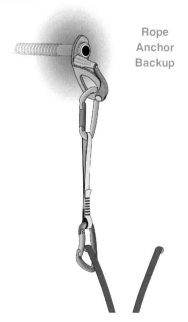

Cord
Anchor
Backup

Rope
Anchor
Backup

Anchors

Snow Bollard

A snow bollard is simple a snow anchor that can be used for abseiling. It would be the last choice when a rock or ice anchor is unavailable.

Step 1

Scribe out a horseshoe shape in the snow, with the opening pointing in the direction of loading. It is usually best to make this about 2.5m at its widest point, but the size depends on the strength of the snow. In very hard snow, the bollard may only need to be 1.5m wide. Whereas in very soft snow it might need to be 3m. It is obviously better to make it too big rather than too small.

Be careful to make it a horseshoe shape, not a teardrop. A lot of the strength comes from the opening as it joins the snowpack. You are not aiming to make an isolated shape.

Step 2

Using the adze of your axe, cut a slot along the scribed line to form a horseshoe shaped trench. This trench should be a minimum of 30cm deep and should be in the firmest layer of snow. Be careful if digging deeper into softer snow because there is the danger that the rope could cut through the soft layer under the bollard.

Step 3

Put the rope over the bollard, making sure it sits well at the bottom of the trench. Check carefully that when the rope is weighted, it remains at the bottom of the trench all the way around and does not lift at all.

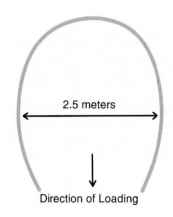

2.5 meters

Direction of Loading

Top View

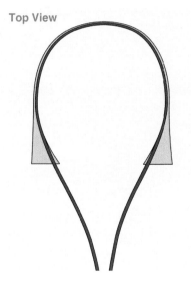

Side View

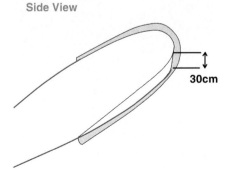

30cm

Anchors

Step 4

Try to test the bollard by committing your weight to it before the situation is consequential.

Step 5

Be very cautious when abseiling, particularly at the start. It is important to stay very low as the rope must not accidentally be pulled in a more upwards direction.

It is often best to start the abseil on your knees or slither on your side to keep the load angle as low as possible.

Multiple People

If multiple people are weighting the anchor, it should be reinforced. Slot one or two axes vertically between the rope and the bollard.

If only one axe is available, it should be at the back of the bollard. With two axes, place them at 10 o'clock and 2 o'clock as shown on the right. This reinforcement can then be removed by the last person to use the anchor.

Important

- Do not disturb the snow in the bollard or immediately in front of it.
- The horseshoe shape should be a smooth curve — sharp angles are weak points.
- It is important that the bollard is slightly incut to prevent the rope rolling up and off.

Frozen Rope

The rope can occasionally become stuck around the bollard if it freezes or becomes buried in spindrift snow. The last person to abseil must check this.

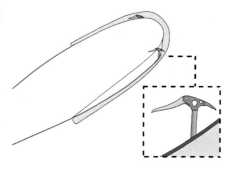

Anchors

Crevasse rescue training near Chamonix, France. Mike Thomas.

Crevasse Rescue Systems

Crevasse Rescue for a Team of Two

Imagine you are travelling on a glacier as a team of two, and your partner in front suddenly disappears down into the snow.

Step 1
The first and most important thing is to hold the fall. This will not be easy!

The best technique is to dig the sides of your feet into the snow (imagine a tug of war type action), while plunging the shaft of your axe into the snow.

If you end up being dragged along the surface, the self arrest position (see page 38) will hopefully stop you as the rope cuts into the lip of the crevasse and increases friction.

Crevasse Rescue

Step 2

After holding the initial fall, kick a secure platform for your downhill foot, or cut one with your axe. This will give you a bit more security to hold the weight while you are making the anchor.

Shout to your partner and check they are okay. It might be very difficult for you to hear them but it's worth trying. If your partner is uninjured and capable of prusiking up the rope or climbing out of the crevasse then that would be the best solution.

Step 3

If you cannot communicate with your partner or they are unable to climb/prusik out by themselves, then you will continue.

Make the appropriate anchor depending on snow condition (see chapter 5). This will be difficult because you are also holding the weight of your partner on the rope.

The anchor needs to be very good, so don't rush it. Be precise and get it right.

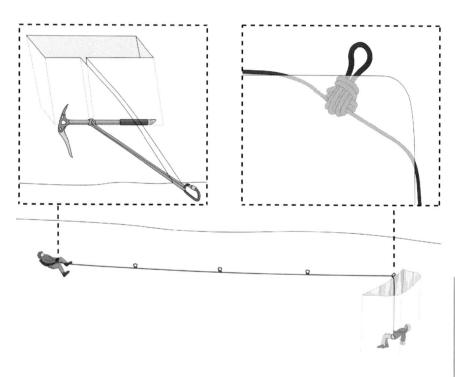

Crevasse Rescue

Step 4

Once the anchor is built, put a French prusik on the weighted rope and then clip this to the newly created anchor (using a micro traxion is better if you have one — see next page).

Push the prusik forward along the rope in front of you. Cautiously allow the weight to pass from you on to the anchor, watching carefully to see if it is working correctly.

Using a Prusik at the Anchor

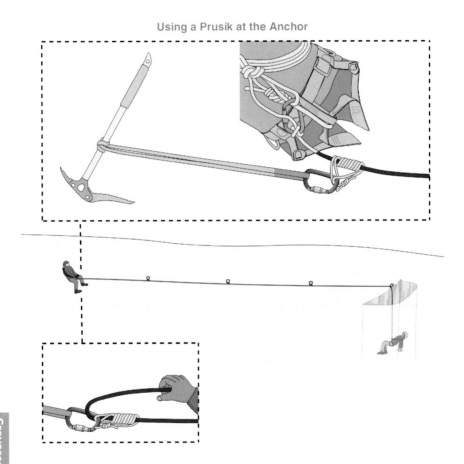

Step 5
(If Using a Prusik at the Anchor)

Clip the unweighted strand of rope through the same carabiner that the prusik is on, ideally this should be a small screwgate orientated so that the narrow end is pointing towards the crevasse.

This now creates an 'autoblock' — meaning that as the rope is pulled through, it locks to capture the progress. This setup generates a lot more friction (which makes hauling more difficult) than using a micro traxion or other type of pulley, but is simple and works.

Crevasse Rescue

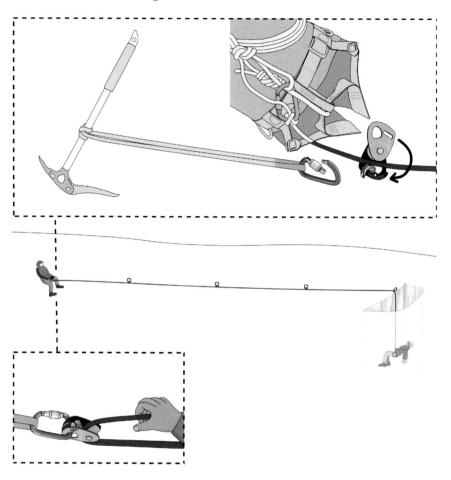

Communication

Communication with the casualty is critical in all of these systems.

Often this is only possible by creating an anchor and having one person move to the lip of the crevasse, or by having a second independent rope team acting as a communication relay.

Crevasse Rescue

Step 6

Tie an overhand knot in the slack rope to act as a backup in case the prusik/pulley slips.

Step 7

Tie a classic prusik on the weighted rope and connect it to your harness. This is to protect you in case you fall into another crevasse but also acts as a backup in case your snow anchor starts to fail.

You can now remove all of your chest coils, but remain tied in to the end of the rope.

Step 8

Move down the weighted rope towards the lip of the crevasse, sliding the prusik as you go. If there are jamming knots in the rope, you'll need to pass them (see next page).

Be very cautious as you approach the lip of the crevasse at this point and keep the prusik behind you to protect yourself from falling in. Check if your partner is okay. If they are fine but cannot prusik out, you will need to haul them.

If your partner is severely injured or unconscious it might be necessary to prusik or abseil down to them and administer emergency first aid or call for rescue services. Never haul an unconscious casualty!

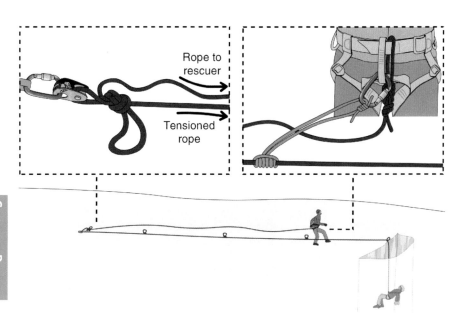

Rope to rescuer

Tensioned rope

If You Need to Walk Past Jamming Knots

To pass a jamming knot while moving towards the crevasse, clip into its loop, then move the prusik over to the next section of rope. Repeat as necessary.

A much quicker (but more dangerous) method is to walk past all the jamming knots first and then attach your prusik. This does not offer a backup for the snow anchor and if you fall into a crevasse, the anchor would be shock-loaded.

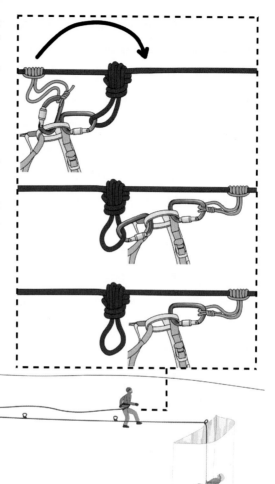

Step 9

Clear the edge of the crevasse. The rope will have cut a slot through into the lip. If it has gone deep, you will need to clear and cut the lip of the crevasse, being careful not to knock anything big onto your partner below.

Pad underneath the rope with walking poles to prevent the rope cutting further into the lip while you are hauling.

Step 10

Move back from the edge of the lip. Clovehitch the slack rope into your harness and unclip from the prusik.

Take the rope which now runs between your harness and the anchor and clip it to the prusik as shown on the next page. This is now a 3:1 hauling system.

Crevasse Rescue

Step 11

Using the power in your legs, claw your way back up to the anchor. As you do this, pull down on the dead rope coming from the back side of the pulley to increase efficiency.

Pull in a straight line with one leg either side of the ropes.

Step 12

Stop just before you reach the anchor and allow the weight to transfer from your harness back to the autoblock/pulley.

Do not continue to move past the anchor as you may disturb the snow which provides its strength.

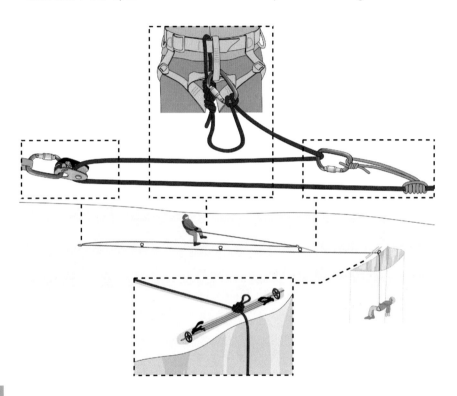

Step 13

Repeat the hauling process as needed. Move back towards the crevasse, adjusting the clovehitch on your harness as you go.

Then adjust the prusik back towards the lip to reset the system.

Step 14

The final stage is to get your partner over the lip of the crevasse. They will probably be stuck if the rope has cut in. Don't just keep pulling, as it is possible to cause injury. If they can't climb out themselves, you will have to go to the lip and help them. Tie yourself in tight and give them a hand, or throw a loop of rope for them to pull on.

Hauling Past Jamming Knots

If you have tied jamming knots in the rope, it will be necessary to deal with them when hauling.

Step 1
Haul as described on the previous pages, but stop when the first jamming knot is 10cm away from the pulley.

Step 2
Attach a 30cm sling to the anchor. Put a French prusik on the weighted rope below the jamming knot and connect it to the sling.

Step 3
Pull with your harness again to free the pulley so that the weight can be transferred onto the prusik.

Step 4
With the weight now removed from the jamming knot, untie it and pull the slack rope through.

Step 5
Remove the sling, prusik and carabiners and continue hauling as normal. Repeat this process for each jamming knot.

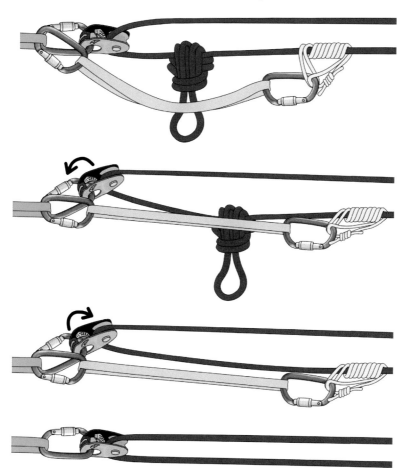

Crevasse Rescue

Crevasse Rescue as a Team of Three or Four

Holding the initial fall is easier with more climbers on the surface to share the weight. The rescue principles are the same as described on the previous pages, but the situation is easier to deal with.

Step 1

The middle climber holds the weight, while the back climber moves forward. As they move forward, they should reduce the slack rope by attaching a prusik and sliding it along.

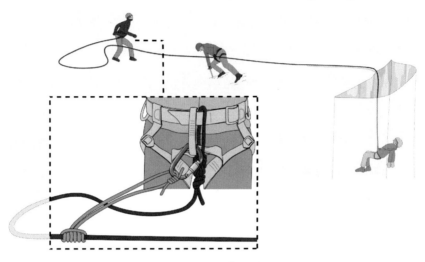

Step 2

The back climber moves in front of the middle climber and constructs an anchor.

Step 3

Once the weight is transferred to the anchor, the system is the same as for a team of two.

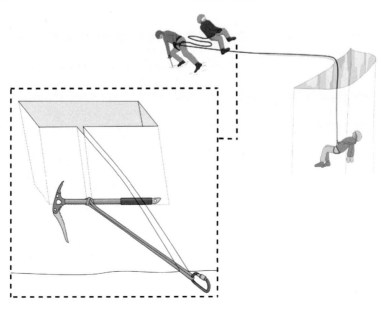

Step 4

The climber who built the anchor should attach to it and sit in a braced position. This protects them and also creates a backup for the anchor. They can then help to haul from their braced position.

Teams of Four

These steps can be modified for a team of four, with an extra climber to assist with hauling or taking some of the strain from the anchor.

Prusiking Out of a Crevasse

Falling into the dark, icy depths of a crevasse sounds like a scene from a bad movie or a worse nightmare.

But this is a real risk when travelling across a glacier, so you'll need to know how to get up to the surface.

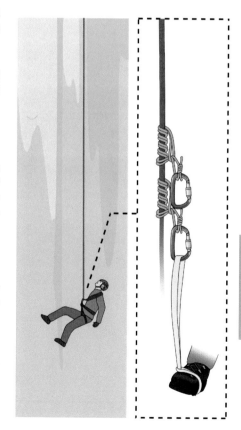

Step 1

Imagine you are hanging in free space in your harness. Start by attaching both prusiks to the rope using klemheist knots and clip carabiners to them.

Step 2

Clip the 120cm sling to the lower klemheist and girth-hitch the other end around your foot.

You may wish to shorten this sling a bit by simply tying an overhand knot in it, so that your knee is bent.

Step 3
Lift your foot and slide both prusiks up the rope as far as you can.

Step 4
Stand up in the sling by tucking your foot underneath and pressing up with your leg while pulling up with your arms at the same time.

Step 5
Clip the top prusik to your belay loop and push it up so there is a gap between the two prusiks. Sit back in your harness so that your weight is hanging from the top prusik.

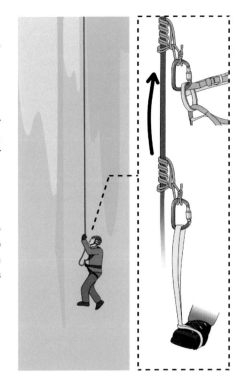

Step 6
Lift your foot again and slide the lower prusik up as high as it will go. Keep repeating this process.

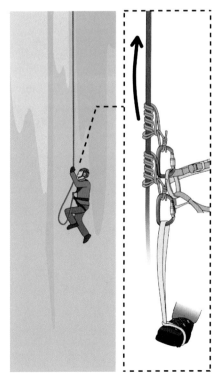

Crevasse Rescue

Back it Up

When you have climbed up the rope enough to generate a loop of slack, you should attach the rope to your harness with a clovehitch. This acts as a backup in case the prusiks fail.

Sliding the Prusik

You may find it awkward to slide a prusik after it has been weighted. To loosen it up, flick open the strand that crosses the knot with your thumb.

Skis

If you are wearing skis, take them off and attach them to your harness by girth-hitching a sling around them, between the bindings.

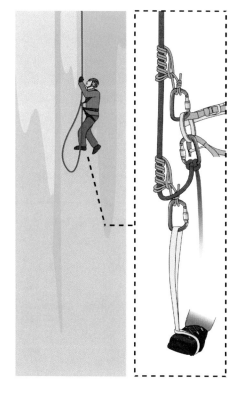

Prusiking Past Jamming Knots

To pass a jamming knot, clip into it as a backup and then re-tie your prusiks one at a time above it.

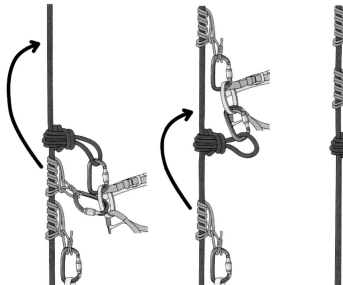

Crevasse Rescue

Ball Glacier, Aoraki Mount Cook National Park, New Zealand. Petrouchka Steiner-Grierson

Essential Knots

Essential Knots

This chapter introduces the most commonly used knots for glacier travel and crevasse rescue. Every climber should be able to recognize, tie and untie the following knots without having to think about it.

Remember that you may have to tie them in situations which are far from ideal and you will trust your life to every knot.

Each knot has multiple uses and, in most cases, there are many knots you could tie to achieve the same result. Before choosing a knot, consider the following. In order of importance:

1) Is it suitable for the intended use?
2) Could it slip or roll?
3) Is it easy to untie or adjust?

Diameter, Flexibility and Surface Friction

The examples given in this manual assume that you are tying identical sections of cord or rope together.

Knots work best when every rope involved is of the same diameter, flexibility, elasticity and surface friction.

Minor differences are fine. For example, tying a 9.5mm and a 10.2mm dynamic rope end-to-end for abseiling is safe. But tying a 6mm tag line to a 10.2mm rope with the same knot will probably result in that knot falling apart.

Likewise, a knot joining an old, stiff static rope to a slick, flexible dynamic rope is likely to slip, even if they are the same diameter.

Dressing

After tying any knot, it is important that you dress it correctly. This means tightening each strand and adjusting the loops and twists so they are perfectly aligned.

Your knots should look exactly like the diagrams in this manual. A knot which isn't well dressed could slip or fail.

Figure-8 Tie In

Uses

The figure-8 is widely accepted as being the safest knot to tie-in with.

Step 1

Make a loop about a meter from the end of the rope. Wrap the end of the rope around the base of the loop, then push the end through as shown.

Step 2

You should end up with an '8'. Make sure the knot is around 90cm from the end of the rope (the exact length varies with ropes of different diameters).

Step 3

Pass the end of the rope through **both** of the two points on the front centre of your harness — the same ones your belay loop runs through. It is important that the rope goes through your harness in exactly the same way as your belay loop does.

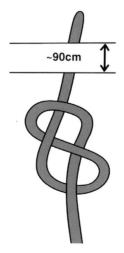

~90cm

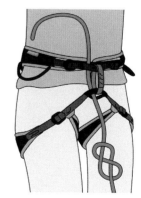

Knots

Step 4
Use the end of the rope to re-trace the figure-8. Follow the twists of the rope starting from where it joins your harness.

Step 5
Continue following the twists until you end up back at the start of the knot.

Pull the whole thing tight.

Step 6
Make sure the end of the rope is around 25cm long. If it is shorter, you'll have to untie and start again. After this, you will need to tie a stopper knot. Loop the short section of rope around the main length.

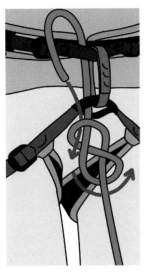

Step 7
Do this twice, with the second loop closer to you than the first.

Step 8
Push the end of the rope through these two loops, away from you.

Step 9
Pull this tight too (make sure it's pushed right up to your figure-8 knot).

Knots

One-Handed Clovehitch

It's often more secure to attach to an anchor while holding onto it with one hand.

Step 1
Clip a screwgate to the anchor and spin it so the gate faces outwards.

Step 2
Hold on to the anchor with one hand so the carabiner is held steady and clip the rope through the carabiner with your other hand.

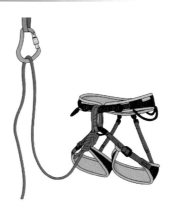

Step 3
If the gate of the carabiner faces right, use your right hand for this step. If it faces left, use your left hand. Reach over the rope at the front and grab the rope at the back with your thumb pointing downwards.

Step 4
Bring the rope forward and twist it so your thumb is upwards.

Step 5
With an extra little twist, push it through the gate of the carabiner and pull it tight.

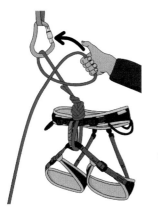

Knots

Girth Hitch (Lark's Foot)

Uses
- Attaching slings to your belay loop.
- Fastening a sling around a snow anchor, such as a ski.

- Attaching slings together.
- Connecting a sling to a carabiner without opening the gate.

Step 1
Feed a sling through your belay loop.

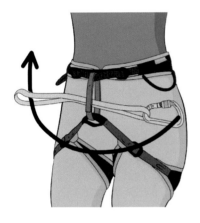

Step 2
Put one end of the sling through the other.

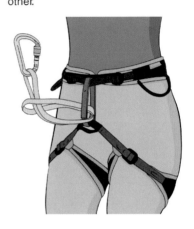

Step 3
Pull it tight.

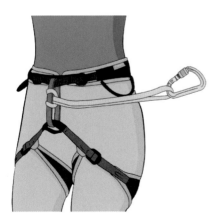

Strop Bend
You can also link two slings together using these same steps.

Arrange the girth hitch as shown below to create a strop bend. This is basically a neater version of the girth hitch.

Knots

Double Fisherman's Bend

Uses
- Tying two ends of cord together to make a prusik or cordelette.

Step 1
Loop one end of the cord around twice as shown to create two loops. Then push the end through these loops.

Spare Cord

Step 2
Pull it tight and do the same with the other end of the cord.

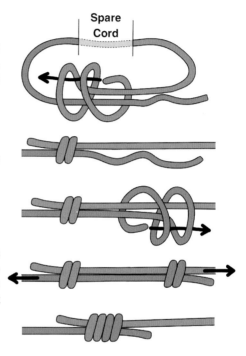

Step 3
Pull it all tight so that the two knots jam together. Make sure the tails are at least 10 times the diameter of the cord (e.g: 5cm tails for a 5mm prusik cord).

Triple Fisherman's Bend

Add an extra coil to make a triple fisherman's bend.

Some slippery cords (such as dyneema) require a triple so they don't slide apart under load — check the manufacturer's recommendations.

Knots

Prusik Knots: Different Types Explained

A prusik is a short piece of cord which can be wrapped around your climbing rope to add friction. They can slide up and down easily, but lock around the rope when weighted.

Prusiks are most commonly used for abseiling but are also incredibly useful in a variety of crevasse rescue situations.

Three types of prusik knot are described on the following pages:
- Classic
- French
- Klemheist

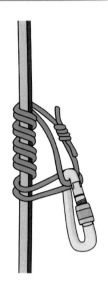

Prusik Cords: Size and Material

Size
The diameter of your cord should be 60% to 80% of the rope's diameter, whether you are using the prusik on one rope or two.

If you use a cord that is too thin, it will cinch tight around the rope when weighted and be difficult to move freely. If you use a cord that is too thick, it won't have enough friction to lock up when you need it to.

In general, 6mm cord works well on 10mm ropes, whereas 5mm cord is better for 8mm ropes.

The cord length should be 1.2m - 1.5m.

Material
Prusiks are usually made out of nylon cord, tied together with a double fisherman's bend.

If the cord is too stiff, it won't lock properly around the rope. The stiffness may also make it difficult to create the knot itself. Test your cord before you take it climbing so you can be sure that it works.

If you are planning to use your prusiks frequently, you should consider buying some pre-sewn prusik loops. These come in a variety of forms, either without a bulky knot or with the knot sewn together and covered by a plastic sleeve.

Knots

Prusik Types: The Classic Prusik

Advantages
- Very secure when loaded.
- Locks in both directions.

Best Uses
- In situations where you need a prusik to lock in either direction.

Disadvantages
- Often difficult to release when tightly loaded.

Step 1
Pass the cord around the rope and through itself as shown, making sure the double fisherman's bend is at the end.

Step 2
Pass the cord around the rope and through itself again.

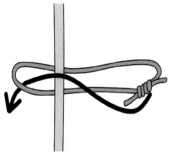

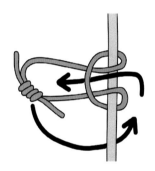

Step 3
Make at least three wraps around the rope, pull the cord tight and clip a carabiner through the loop.

Make sure the knot is neat.

Step 4
Weight the knot in either direction to lock it. Pinch the knot to loosen it. This allows you to move it up or down the rope. If the knot gets stuck, you can push some cord in from the center of the knot to loosen it.

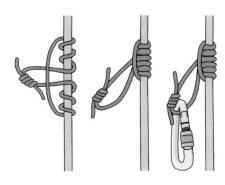

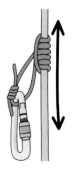

Knots

Prusik Types: The French Prusik

Advantages
- Easy to tie and untie.
- Can be released under load.

Best Uses
- As a back-up when abseiling.

Disadvantages
- Tends to slip when used to ascend ropes.

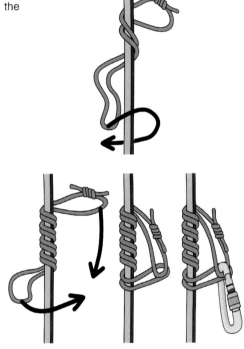

Step 1
Wrap the prusik neatly around the rope a few times as shown.

Step 2
Clip the ends together with a carabiner. More wraps will create more friction around the ropes, though four wraps are generally enough.

Make sure the wraps are neat and the double fisherman's bend is away from the ropes.

Step 3
Pinch the knot to loosen it. This allows you to move it down the rope.

Weight the knot to lock it. The French prusik locks in both directions, but the double fisherman's bend tends to wrap itself into the prusik when the direction is switched, making it much less effective.

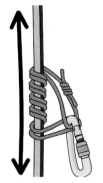

Knots

Prusik Types: The Klemheist Knot

Advantages
- Easy to release after being loaded.
- Can be tied with webbing.

Best Uses
- Ascending a rope.

Disadvantages
- Only works in one direction.

Step 1
Wrap the prusik neatly around the rope a few times as shown.

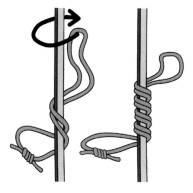

Step 2
Pass the end of the cord through the loop.

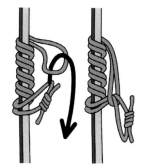

Step 3
Attach a carabiner.

Weight the knot downwards to lock it, or push it upwards to release.

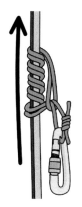

Knots

Prusik Cord Tips

* Prusiks are not full-strength attachment points. Always have a back-up so you're attached to the rope 'properly'.

* The number of wraps should be increased or decreased depending on the cord stiffness, cord diameter and moisture conditions, with three wraps as a minimum. Before using any prusik knot, test it to see if it grips and releases well.

* If you don't have a prusik cord, you can use a sling instead. Slings don't work quite as well but it'll help you get out of a tricky situation. A narrow nylon sling is better than Dyneema (Spectra). Don't use a sling for anything except a prusik after using it once as a prusik.

* Make sure not to wrap the double fisherman's bend into any friction hitch. This will greatly decrease the knot's effectiveness.

* If using prusiks in conditions where they might fail (e.g; prusiking up a wet or icy rope), it's better to use two different types of prusik (and a full strength back-up, of course). If conditions exist to cause one to slip or fail, the likelihood is that the other prusik would not fail under the same conditions.

* Check your prusik cord for wear and tear regularly. Make sure the double fisherman's bend isn't slipping and the cord isn't abraded. When it's looking worn, retire it and get a new one — cord is cheap.

Knots

Other VDiff Titles

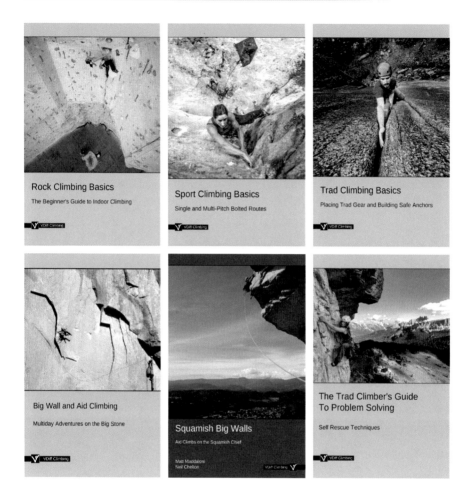

Rock Climbing Basics
The Beginner's Guide to Indoor Climbing

Sport Climbing Basics
Single and Multi-Pitch Bolted Routes

Trad Climbing Basics
Placing Trad Gear and Building Safe Anchors

Big Wall and Aid Climbing
Multiday Adventures on the Big Stone

Squamish Big Walls
Aid Climbs on the Squamish Chief
Matt Maddaloni
Neil Chelton

The Trad Climber's Guide To Problem Solving
Self Rescue Techniques

Having the knowledge of safe climbing skills is the lightest and most useful equipment you can take on any climb.

Learn before you go. Don't actually take these books up there with you!

Available as paperbacks or e-books. For more information, visit:
www.vdiffclimbing.com

Index

Notes

Notes

Notes

Notes

Made in the USA
Las Vegas, NV
25 November 2023

81517640R00052